Waiting for Joey

An Antarctic Penguin Journal

Jean Pennycook

The Lexile Framework for Reading ® Lexile measure ® 1040L

For further information, contact:

Tumblehome, Inc.
201 Newbury St, Suite 201
Boston, MA 02116
http://www.tumblehomelearning.com

Library of Congress Control Number: 2018947129
ISBN 978-1-943431-41-0 (hardcover)
ISBN 978-1-943431-45-8 (paperback)

Pennycook, Jean
Waiting for Joey / Jean Pennycook - 1st ed, 2nd print

Design: Yu-Yi Ling

Printed in Taiwan

10 9 8 7 6 5 4 3 2 1

This book is dedicated to the members of my research team, who have worked in the harshest environment on earth for 3 decades trying to unravel the mysteries of the Ross Seas ecosystem.

And to my family, Carson, Graham, Harper and Declan, for seventeen lost Christmases.

ANTARCTICA FACTS

The fifth largest continent is almost completely (98%) covered with ice and therefore supports no land animals. The average depth of ice is 1.9 km (1.2 mi) and at the geographical South Pole, it is 2700m (9000 ft).

Among Earth's seven continents, Antarctica is on average the:
- highest, average 2500 m (8200ft)
- coldest, average cold in winter −63°C (−81°F)
- driest, average 200 mm (8 inches) precipitation near the coast, much less inland
- windiest, highest recorded 327km/h (199 mph), average 20 km/h (12.3mph)

The continent is surrounded by the Southern Ocean.

There is no record of an indigenous population; however, between 4000-5000 scientists come to the continent every year in about 78 research stations.

The temperature range at Cape Royds is -18°F to 33°F. The Sun sets at 1:32pm on April 24 and does not rise again until 12:23pm on August 19. During the Antarctic summer from October 23 to February 20 the sun never sets. This is the time frame for this story about Joey and when most science takes place.

Chapter 1

Joey (2008)

I fly seventeen hours from Los Angeles to Christchurch, New Zealand, then eight more on a military cargo jet. A smooth landing on a runway made of ice and I am in Antarctica. Stepping off the plane, taking my first breath of Antarctic cold, my lungs revolt as frigid air enters my body. Icy wind finds every opening in my clothes, and my skin is in shock. I am not prepared for this onslaught from the frozen environment and wonder, *Have I made a mistake in coming?*

It is all new and I am excited to be joining Dr. David Ainley and his Adélie penguin research team at Cape Royds on Ross Island in Antarctica. Our mission is to learn as much about these remarkable birds as we can in three short months. Dr. Ainley has been coming here for thirty years, and many of the team members have more than a decade of experience. I feel like the new girl in the class, and luckily there are still mysteries to solve.

Antarctica is a wonderland—remote, eternally frozen, and isolated, but spectacular in its scenery and wildlife. It is both exciting and a bit scary to be reborn into this new career. For the last twenty years, I have taught science to high school students; now I will be unraveling the mysteries of Adélie penguins on a grant from the National Science Foundation. We have much to learn; me the most of all! Our research focuses on how penguins are coping with alterations in their environment due to climate and ecosystem change. Studying these changes requires that we live in a tent near the nesting birds for two and a half months. Over time, these birds have mastered survival in this environment with elegance, confidence, and grace. They represent an evolutionary success. We will observe their resiliency and adaptation to changes in their habitat, lessons that humans may need to learn as our environments are changing as well.

Our living and working tent is up the hill and far enough away that we cannot hear the nonstop squabbling, bickering, and quarreling for nesting space, rocks, and mates among the more than 4,000 Adélie penguins in the colony. In our camp, there is no running water, so there will be no shower, no way to wash clothes. The outfit I am wearing the day I arrive will be the same outfit I will wear the day I leave. A solar panel provides only enough electricity for computers, cameras,

Cape Royds Hut

and emergency radios. No microwave, coffee maker, TV, or toaster. We cook meals on a small two-burner propane camp stove. We sleep in a tent with no heat and we pee into a bucket. Although this living seems minimal, I am amazed at the amount of equipment, gear, and support required for me to survive even one day in this environment. These 5-kilogram (11-pound) birds that come up to my knee clearly are better able to survive in this place than I, and they only have a layer of fat and the feathers on their backs, plus their instincts.

Sleep tent

My first season working at Cape Royds is full of unknowns as I watch penguin parents frantic to build nests, lay eggs, and raise chicks, all within the short window of summer that this harsh land allows. I am awkward and uneasy in my new job, but thrilled to take on the challenge of living and working with penguins in their environment. I learn how to observe penguin behavior and record what they eat. We catch, weigh, and measure penguin chicks to compare growth rates and keep track of their progress as we watch them become independent of their parents. As eggs hatch, I watch new life fight its way into an unforgiving world by breaking out of the protective shell where it has been sheltered for thirty-two days. I learn to accept predation, starvation, abandonment, and loss as daily events in a penguin breeding colony. These events deeply sadden me, but the frenzied pace of penguin life doesn't slow down. No time for grief or mourning: the breeding season is short, and there is no room for error or hesitation in this cycle of life.

The season passes quickly, and I relate to the Adélie chicks as they learn to navigate the rules of penguin life. I, too, am developing new skills. The last task of the research season is to band 200 of the chicks at our colony just before they fledge, heading into the ocean for the first time. The bands, which are numbered, are shaped like an airplane wing in cross section, so as not to interfere with swimming. We bend the band around the top of a penguin's wing with our thumbs. The selected birds will wear the bands for the rest of their lives, allowing us to identify them in the future. Our team monitors three of the several penguin breeding colonies in the Ross Sea, and we will search for these identified birds in the coming years. Having a life history of individual birds is an important part of understanding their lives and how they make changes as the environment changes around them.

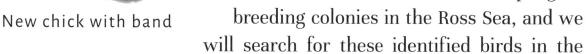

New chick with band

It takes a special strength of the thumbs to bend the band for a perfect fit, and I am slower than the seasoned team members. The others are packing up while I still have a few bands to go. Finally, with one band left in my pocket, I approach the last, smallest chick in the corral. I consider leaving this male chick out of our study,

since he may be too small and weak to survive the first winter. I ponder my choice. Should I band him or go catch another, more robust chick? But that would take more time. The team is waiting for me to finish. Gently, I hold the fragile, squirming chick and attach the band to his flipper—#1050—then give him a pat and let him go. As he dashes off to join the other chicks, he looks back at me with bright-eyed interest in his new life. I name him Joey... and wonder if I will ever see him again, what his life will be like, and where he will go next.

Many of the parents have already left for the season, but Joey and the other chicks must wait until they have lost their chick feathers and grown adult plumage before they can enter the ocean and find food. The first-year coat of feathers will mark them as subadults. They are blue and white rather than black and white, and will have a white chin and a black rather than white eyering. No longer dependent chicks, they will be on their own.

Joey

GET TO KNOW ADÉLIE PENGUINS

Common name	Adélie penguin
Scientific name	Pygoscelis adeliae
Classification	Animalia – Chordata – Aves – Spenisciformes – Pygoscelis – adeliae
Closest relatives	Chinstrap and Gentoo penguins
Average life	11-21 years
Height	18-26 inches (70cm)
Weight	8-13 lbs (3-7kg)
Food	fish, krill, squid. Usually 164-229 feet (50-70 m) dives but can go as far as 575 feet (175 m) down.
Habitat	pack ice around the entire coast of Antarctica
Breeding	on land between Oct-Jan (austral summer). Build nest out of rocks. Lay 2 eggs which take 32-34 days to hatch.

HOW DO WE KNOW WHAT WE KNOW

Where do Adélie Penguins go for food? How far do they have to go? How long does it take? How deep do they dive and how many dives do they make? These are very important questions to answer so we can work to protect the feeding grounds of these special birds. It is not enough to just protect their breeding ground, we need to set aside part of the ocean as well and keep humans from taking their food. We attach trackers (pp.25, 26) to their feathers, which is similar to putting a clip in your hair and does not hurt them. They wear it for only a few days and bring back the data to answer all the questions above.

Chapter 2

My Second Season (2009)

The off-season (the months between seasons on the ice) has passed quickly. I spent the time rethinking what to pack, getting a new camera, and learning tricks of the trade for our project website. I am a veteran now—my luggage is lighter, my equipment weatherproof. Meals will be more varied now that I have learned new ways to cook on a camp stove. I have brought a better set of warm underwear, a thicker jacket, a second hat, stronger shoes, enough of my favorite coffee, extra chocolate, and spare batteries for my camera. Setting up camp feels routine: I easily move through chores and project activities, and I can put up my tent by myself. I think of Joey also learning the skills he needs to be a penguin in the Ross Sea, keeping warm, finding food, avoiding crashing ice floes, and staying away from predators.

Nest with male

By late October, we are back at Cape Royds, and the penguins have started to return. The males come first to establish their territory, gather rocks, and build their nests. A good nest is one that will help attract a female to share the burden of rearing chicks. The large bowl shape of the nest keeps eggs and small chicks in place and above any melt water. Often a male will wait for his mate from last year, but time is short and if she does not show up promptly, he will select a new female. Females have a timeline of their own. Eggs form in their bodies as they work their way to the colony, so finding a mate soon after they arrive is critical. Eggs need to be fertilized if they are going to hatch. Each female needs to find a suitable nest and a mate so that her chicks survive.

This year, our team is determining how much food it takes to raise an Adélie penguin chick. We build a fence around one of the breeding groups (about thirty-five nests) and create a single opening for the penguins to enter and exit their nesting area. When the chicks are small, parents take turns staying on the nest. While one adult keeps the chicks warm and protects them from predation, the other adult walks to the open ocean, feeds itself, and then fills its belly with food for the chicks.

We implant some of the nesting adults with small electronic chips under the skin on their backs. These are similar to the ones put into pets for identification. When the penguins leave the area, they go through a gate and walk over a scale. The gate and scale are connected to a computer in a tent

nearby. The computer reads the chip to identify the bird and records the weight of the penguin when it leaves and again when it comes back. By subtracting the first from the second weight, we know how much food the parent is bringing back to the chicks. We also know how long it takes the parents to find and capture their prey. Our data show it takes about 28 kilograms (61.7 pounds) of food to raise an Adélie chick to fledging weight,

Weighbridge

which is 3–4 kilograms (6.6–8.8 pounds). Most foraging trips take less than a day at the small Royds colony.

It is extremely rare for a one-year-old Adélie penguin to return to the breeding colony. Young Adélies spend their first few years at sea, eating, maturing, and learning how to be penguins. They learn how to outmaneuver their predators—leopard seals and killer whales—in the water. Exactly where young penguins spend their first years out in the Ross Sea is still unknown, but we believe they stay in areas of ocean largely covered with massive pieces of sea ice, called ice floes. In the same way that other birds live in trees, Adélie penguins live on these ice floes. Their food of fish and krill lives under the ice floes, which move with the winds, tides, and currents. The young penguins tend to cluster in small groups of six to seven—whether siblings stay together we do not know.

Leopard seal

When I returned to Cape Royds this October, I did not expect to see Joey, although I looked for him among the groups of penguins that started to waddle ashore and build their nests. As the season progresses, I gain confidence in my ability to work with penguins, weigh chicks, and record nesting behavior. Still, I constantly think of Joey. I wonder where he is and what he is doing. I know he is gaining the skills he will need to survive as an adult Adélie penguin. Alas, the season ends and I'm the one who departs.

15

Chapter 3
Penguin Cam (2010)

Another new season, and my travel path is the same as last year. We have maps and a GPS (global positioning system), and we can see Cape Royds from a distance. We will not get lost. The open ocean is about 5 kilometers (3.1 miles) from the colony, normal for Cape Royds. Penguins prefer to swim, but to get to Cape Royds this year they will have to walk this distance over a continuous sheet of ice. Most people think penguins have short legs, but Adélie penguins have long, strong legs, partly hidden by their body and feathers. They also have sturdy feet and sharp nails to help navigate the slippery sea ice. How they find their way back from their winter feeding grounds in the Ross Sea is not well understood. Sight, smell, clues from the sun, currents, winds, and magnetic lines—all could play a part; the answer is waiting for

Penguin feet

the next group of researchers to uncover. However, today, right on cue, here come the male penguins, first in small groups and then in larger ones. They have navigated hundreds of kilometers in open ocean and over sea ice to their nesting sites at Cape Royds, a feat humans could not accomplish without the help of technology.

The breeding season is short, and penguins cannot waste time. Unlike birds living in warmer climates with longer summers, these penguins are very synchronous in their breeding behavior. This means they all lay their eggs and raise their chicks within a very short time span. Eggs are laid within a two-week window. Hatching occurs in a similar, coordinated pattern, and the chicks need to be fledged by the end of January. Winter comes quickly, and chicks not ready to be on their own will not survive.

Since we do not arrive in the colony until late October, our team has set up an automatic penguin camera (penguin cam) that takes five close-up pictures of the colony every day. This way, we monitor the birds' arrival dates from our warm homes in California. Many adult Adélie penguins will return to Cape Royds after their chicks are gone. They come to molt, a yearly process of shedding old feathers and growing new ones. Molting is essential, as feathers wear out and penguins depend on their feathers to keep them warm and dry. We can watch molting on the penguin cam as well, long after we leave. We do not know where, but by now Joey must have molted. He now wears adult colors, black and white, with a black chin and

Molter

white eye ring. Every year, he will leave last year's feathers behind and start a new set as he grows and matures. In similar fashion, every time I come to Antarctica, I leave my old life behind to experience new things, see new places, and learn new skills.

Cape Royds is the southernmost breeding colony for Adélie penguins. On their way from the wintering areas north of the Ross Sea, Cape Royds penguins pass several other suitable breeding colonies. But perhaps their previous experience and genetic makeup compels them to swim past the others and come here. It takes longer to get here, so they are the last of the colonies to begin the breeding cycle. At our neighboring colony about 40 kilometers (24.9 miles) to the north, the birds begin breeding about a week earlier.

The first arriving penguins at Cape Royds in October are fat, clean, bright, and shiny, as shown in the picture below. The date of arrival, along with other landmark dates, helps

us understand how the colony is doing and if the penguins are making any changes in the timing of their breeding. As climate change alters the sea ice conditions, we are interested in recording these dates. This year, the first egg appears on November 6 and the first chick December 12. These dates are about average for Cape Royds, a few days later than at other colonies on Ross Island.

A few, but not many, two-year-old Adélie penguins come back to the breeding colony, so maybe I'll see Joey this year. I check the banded birds in the colony for his number every day. Many young penguins wander near and within the colony but most stay mainly out on the sea ice, and I check for him there as well. Band numbers tell us what year each penguin was born and in which colony. Other penguins from Joey's birth year show up. I am excited to see some of Joey's classmates, but I do not see Joey. Hopefully, he is out on an ice floe exploring ways to catch fish, looking for the best places for krill and keeping his distance from leopard seals. I am disappointed and wonder if he is still alive. Fifty percent of young birds do not make it to adulthood.

Chapter 4

Skuas (2011)

Another year has passed. Joey is now three years old, and there is a good chance he will return to the colony. Young birds come ashore later in the breeding season, after eggs are laid or even after they begin to hatch, to observe, socialize and learn nest-building skills with other young birds.

Although adult Adélie penguins have no land-based predators in Antarctica, the south polar skuas arrive at Cape Royds to raise their chicks near the penguin colony. These large, gull-like birds are scavengers and wily predators that eat both penguin eggs and chicks left unguarded by their parents. Skuas are long-lived seabirds, and mated pairs appear together over many years in the same nest. This year, there are about eight skua nests near the penguin colony. I check them every day to record when their eggs are laid and chicks hatch.

Skua

Most of the Adélie penguins build their nests just out of pecking range of their neighbors. They don't choose this distance by accident. Any closer and a penguin sitting on the nest would be able to reach its neighbor. Such closeness would result in pecks, jabs, and squawks, as these birds are very territorial and

22

Skua with chick

want to own enough space to interact with their mates or chicks without interference. But any further apart and the skuas would be able to land between nests, giving them greater access to eggs and chicks. Having neighbors close by helps to keep the skuas away. This spacing is just right for both peaceful neighborhoods and protection from attack.

Occasionally, a penguin will build a nest away from the group. Solitary nests are easy pickings for the skuas. Skuas hunt in pairs, which can easily outmatch penguins that build their nest away from the safety of others or chicks that wander away from the protection of their parents. Early in the season, skuas steal eggs; later, they take chicks. Predation is never fun to observe, but it is part of the cycle of life here in Antarctica. Skuas have their own chicks to feed, and young penguins are part of the food chain.

As the chicks get bigger, they demand more food. In about a month, they are

Nesting space

An isolated nest from afar

too big for the nest, so they huddle in small groups called crèches. These groups help keep the chicks warm and also help protect them from the skuas. During this time, both parents are out in the ocean foraging for food. Enough young, nonbreeding, subadult penguins are around to help keep skuas away. A whack from a penguin flipper can easily break a skua's hollow bones. Many two- to five-year-old penguins show up at the colony and take on this role. We watch them build practice nests along the periphery of established nests, gain confidence in the mating routine, and repel any skuas. All season I look for band #1050, but Joey does not show up. Once again, I am disappointed and concerned. Perhaps Joey is still alive but finding other colonies to explore. Less than half of the birds that hatch at Cape Royds will return to make their nests here.

An isolated nest

Chick crèche

Chapter 5

Joey Returns (2012)

This year, our research team takes on a new project. We attach trackers to the backs of nesting adults. After the penguins wear them for a single foraging trip, we download the data and map where they have been, how many dives they took to find food, how deep they dove, and how long they were gone from the nest. The more birds we outfit

Tracker

with these devices, the more information we have. We are learning about penguin feeding behavior. We wonder if there is a difference between the feeding patterns of the males and females, if they always go to the same area, if they stay close to the ice or prefer open water, and how many dives they need to get enough food for themselves and their chicks.

Tracker on penguin's back

Food passage

26

Penguin parents swallow their food whole as they swim in the ocean. Today, I am wandering the colony and recording what comes out of the adults' mouths into the chicks' mouths. We call this regurgitation, and it is how we know what the adult birds are finding to eat in the ocean. In the early days of penguin research about a hundred years ago, researchers killed birds and opened their stomachs to determine what they were eating; the penguins would then be fed to sled dogs. More recently, researchers forced parents to throw up hard-won meals by sticking a tube down their throats. Nowadays, we do not want to interfere with penguins' lives and certainly not to harm them in any way. Instead, we wait patiently for adults to regurgitate food to the chicks. Looking closely through binoculars, we can see the food being passed from parent to chick—gray mush is fish and pink mush is krill. What comes out the other end of these birds adds layers and layers of slippery guano and a haze of digester krill and fish odor to the colony, which is the other reason we camp 400 meters (about 1300 feet) away.

Poop squirt

Regurgitated krill

Today, I sit on a rock close to one of the breeding groups waiting for adults to return from the ocean full of food for their chicks. I look up to see a banded bird waddle into the colony. I notice it, but presuming it must be on its way to an established nest, I decide I'll check its number later. Then, when it wanders close to me, I glance at the number. It's #1050—Joey! He's four years old. I can't help smiling.

The Adélie penguins we work with are not pets. They are wild birds and must stay that way. We do not hold them, feed them, or play with them. Still, I'm filled with joy when I see Joey. All my worries about his survival are over for now. Although he comes close to me and tilts his head to stare, he quickly moves on without hesitation or sign of recognition. I can hardly wait to follow him, see where he wanders, how long he will stay, and what he will do. It is too late in the season to raise

Curious

a family so he may not stay long, so I check on him every day. He spends just six days in the colony, trying to build a nest out of discarded rocks, stealing some from other nests, practicing the mating and territorial call, and spending many hours resting. I am in awe and wonder of that small bird I banded four years ago. He is now a robust young adult, but he will need more time to practice penguin social arts before he can establish himself with a nest, mate, and family.

Territorial call

Chapter 6
Summer Storms (2013)

R eturning to Cape Royds this year includes a challenge—digging out our tent site from deep snow up the hill from the penguins. The good news is that we will have a built-in freezer in the nearby snowbank for the entire season. Our frozen food will stay frozen!

Many Adélie penguins return to within a few centimeters of their exact nest location year after year. This year, snowdrifts have covered the Seaview area, a small nesting group of about fifteen pairs. However, these sturdy birds are not deterred. We watch as, day after day, the males carry rocks to the top of a snowdrift that is 150 centimeters (4.9 feet) high and re-create their nests from last year over the exact same position. What drives the birds to remember their nest site from year to year and to be so precise in their construction is still a mystery, particularly now

Digging out the tent

when their previous territory is covered with all that snow. Shifting just 3 meters (9.8 feet) in any direction would offer these penguins bare ground with plenty of small stones, but they insist on making their nest on top of the snow mound.

I am curious as to how these nests in the snow will survive. It isn't long before the story unravels. As the days go by, the warm penguin bodies melt the snow, and both the nests and the eggs begin to sink into the snowbank. Finally, the eggs end up in the mud, cold and wet. The entire Seaview group fails to hatch even one egg. It is very difficult for me to watch how much work, attention, care, and energy went into building these nests, laying, and brooding the eggs, only to have it all end in muddy disaster.

Snow nests

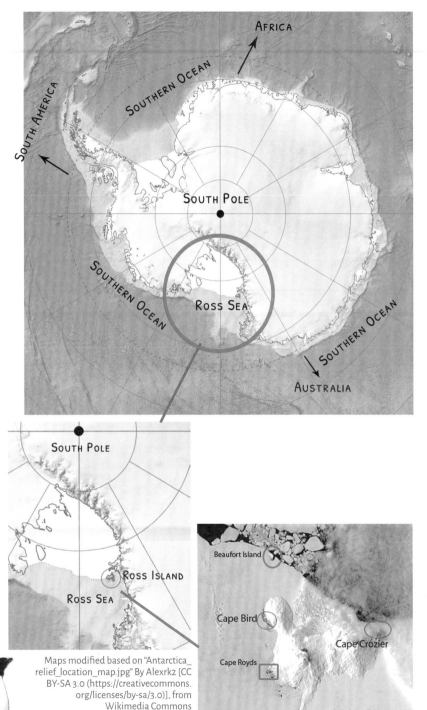

Our team monitors two other Adélie penguin colonies in the Ross Sea region: Cape Bird (70,000 breeding pairs) and Cape Crozier (300,000 pairs). This season, we have team members looking for banded penguins at these other colonies over the course of several months. I'm eager to hear from them, because Joey has not returned to Cape Royds. We have learned that about 10 percent of penguins find their way to different colonies from the ones where they were hatched to build their nests. With a lucky break in both weather and sea ice conditions, we are able to visit a fourth colony, Beaufort Island. A thirty-minute helicopter ride away, Beaufort Island has no science stations and is only accessible by boat or helicopter. We look for penguins from our other three colonies to see if they have made a home there. Some of them have. I look for Joey everywhere, but he is not among the Beaufort Island birds.

The heavy snowfall this year continues. Penguins are used to the Antarctic cold and summer storms. They are determined to stay on eggs and chicks no matter what the weather, even when the snow piles up around them. We watch as this happens to a small group of nests near the colony entrance called the Snow Group. As the heavy storms of this year pile up the snow, the adults on the nests hold their wings above their heads to keep breathing holes open. In some cases, only the tip of the parent penguin's beak is visible. In others, the bird could not get out of the snow and has perished. Where we can, we use our hands to dig the birds out and are able to save several adults, but many eggs and chicks are lost.

Birds in snow cave

As our global climate warms, there is more evaporation from the oceans. As this moist air moves over the cold land, water vapor condenses, and heavy rain or snow fall. Summer storms this year at Cape Royds are more severe due to extra moisture in the atmosphere, and the penguins have difficulty coping. In the warmer Antarctic Peninsula, further north and close to South America, snowfall is increasing dramatically. It doesn't melt in time for the Adélie penguins to begin nesting early enough in the season. Thus, these penguins' breeding population is shifting farther south where it doesn't snow as much.

Breathing hole

Throughout this season, I wait for Joey and ask our team members at both Cape Bird and Cape Crozier if they have seen him. He was here last year, and I was hoping he would return, but nobody spots him anywhere. I can only hope he went to a different colony outside the Ross Island area or just spent the summer in safety out on the sea ice.

Chapter 7
Raising Penguin Chicks Is Hard
(2014)

This year, Joey is six years old. If he is still alive, I am optimistic he will return to Cape Royds to make a go at nest building and chick rearing. Starting the moment I arrive in camp, I look for him every day. And then, on October 30, there he is! Joey is sleek, fat, and here early in the season. This is a good start. I can't wait to watch and see what unfolds for him. At first, he wanders a bit, and then he settles on a site near where he was raised as a chick. Several nests are already being built. Joey selects a place near the edge and starts to bring rocks one at a time, carrying them in his beak. After three days,

Carrying a stone for nest construction

Joey's nest is complete, and he begins the courtship display. A few females wander by; two of them stop and inspect the nest, then move on. Joey does not give up but instead collects more rocks and displays to every female that passes. His call and his well-built nest let the females know he is a worthy mate to help raise chicks. At last, a female stops and stays. Joey and his mate learn each other's unique song, which will let them find and recognize each other for the rest of the season. I am delighted to hear the song sung as a duet and overjoyed six days later to see two eggs in the nest. It is November 12.

Producing and laying eggs requires an expenditure of energy. At the beginning of the nesting process, the penguins remain at the colony for a week or two without eating, so they lose weight. After depositing their eggs, females return to the ocean to feed, while the males take the first turn on the nest. Males have an extra layer of body fat when they arrive in the colony, as they won't feed for a while. Antarctica is cold and windy, and the skuas lurk close by. Eggs need to be covered at all times with the warmth and protection of an adult penguin's body. Sometimes the females are away foraging for up to two weeks. The males have gone without food or water since arriving in the colony.

There is no sign of Joey's mate ten days after she left. Joey has been in the colony for more than three weeks, which is a long time without food or water. Thankfully, his female appears on the eleventh day and trades places on the nest with Joey. It is November 23. Now it is his turn to head to the ocean for food. He must be very hungry, but before he leaves he takes the time to bring a few new rocks to the nest and his mate as if to say, "Don't worry, I'll be back." Snow from a nearby snowbank provides a much-needed drink as he works his way to the ocean.

I visit the nest every day. Joey has been gone for a week. By December 1, the eggs are eighteen days old, and I see Joey, fat, clean, and walking with parental determination toward the nest. A joyous duet occurs between the penguin pair as they greet and exchange places. As the female heads off to forage, Joey settles his warm body onto the eggs. It will be another fourteen days before the eggs hatch. This time, the female is gone for only nine days. She, too, returns fat and sleek from eating krill and small fish—the food this year is plentiful. One more time, the recognition song sounds. The pair trade places on the nest, and Joey waddles off to feed. I can only wonder if he knows the eggs will hatch soon.

Two days pass, and when I check the nest, the female is sitting quietly. She doesn't even open her eyes as I walk by, but today the number of skuas in the area troubles me. They seem to be aggressively attacking nests in Joey's breeding group. I stay close for a while, hoping my presence will encourage them to move on. But I have work to do, so I must leave. I will check in later. Two hours go by, and I return to see what I most feared. Both eggs in Joey's nest are gone. The female stands in the middle of the empty pile of rocks, agitated and shaken. I was not there to witness the event, but I know how it happened. Before they lay their own eggs, skua pairs hunt together. One will sit in front of a nesting penguin and tease it with jabs and stabs of the beak. The other swoops in from the side or behind and grab the eggs. It is a sad day. I stay to watch, and in a few minutes Joey's mate settles down on the cold, now eggless nest. She shows no sign of grief or sadness, just acceptance. It is December 12.

Tag team skua

38

2-day old penguin chick

We see the first chicks of the season the next day. New life, increased energy, and noise in the colony make a happy day for us. We find as many chicks as we can, and we note the locations. These will be our oldest chicks of the season. I check on Joey's nest, and his mate is still there. Does she realize the eggs are gone? Is she waiting for Joey? We do not know what the birds think, nor should we speculate. However, by December 15, the female is gone, and most of the rocks have been stolen. It is December 16, the day I would have expected Joey's eggs to hatch, and here comes Joey, his belly full of krill and fish. I see him move quickly through the colony toward his nest. When he arrives, he calls out, but there is no one to sing his song to, no chicks to feed, and only the scant remains of his hard-earned nest. The scene brings tears to my eyes, but Joey, in absolute penguin form, stands for a moment in the nest and then settles down and goes to sleep, no doubt now digesting the food he was bringing to feed his chicks. Four days later, he is gone.

Chapter 8
Fish and Krill (2015)

Every year is a new adventure at Cape Royds. For several years, we have been observing the food that the penguins feed to their chicks. I sit on a rock and watch as the parent regurgitates either a mass of pink (krill) or silver-gray (fish) food into the chick's mouth. Over time, we have noticed that early in the season they feed krill, then switch to fish and back to krill. Why is that so? Does their food source in the ocean change? Do all the breeding colonies of Adélies follow this pattern? Is it a changing nutritional demand of the chicks that the parents are responding to? Is it something we cannot think of?

Our team analyzes data about what is occurring in the ocean and discover that the supply of krill and fish stays about the same throughout the season. It looks like the penguins can find whatever they want.

Our season starts with Joey showing up by October 31. Happily, I watch him build his nest on the same nest site as before. Although not positive, I feel certain he is with the same female as last year. They mate quickly and by November 10, two eggs are laid. For them, the breeding season is underway.

I begin doing Skype calls to classrooms around the country, mostly while sitting next to Joey's nest. We discuss penguin behavior, Antarctica habitat, and penguin adaptations. I introduce Joey to the students. He quickly becomes a celebrity and is featured on our Nest Check page, where more than 300 classrooms follow his progress with daily pictures. One student sends in the name Echo for his mate, and so she is crowned. Some students wonder if I see polar bears. No, there are no polar bears in Antarctica, only in the Arctic. Others ask about how we live in the tent, where we go to the bathroom, or how the research is coming. Some ask how we can tell the penguins apart. The answer: we can't, unless they are banded. I get hundreds of questions during the Skype calls and I'm so happy that students want to connect with penguins in Antarctica.

Joey and Echo

Echo and Joey trade off brooding the eggs and fending off the skuas. Foraging trips are short, as the open ocean is close this year. By December 15, both eggs have hatched. Joey and Echo start feeding their chicks krill, then in a couple of weeks change to fish. Fifteen days later, they change back to krill, just like the other penguin parents.

Brood patch

We are still puzzled at this pattern. Then we look at one other set of data we have been collecting—the presence of minke whales in the area. Every day, we do a whale watch. Someone climbs the peak and for a couple of hours counts the number and type of whales in the area. We see mostly minke whales and killer whales (orcas). Since minkes are krill eaters, they naturally will move to the areas with the highest concentration of krill. Minkes do not bother the penguins, and we frequently see them swimming near each other, but the minkes are aggressive competitors for the penguins' krill supply. The whales have a very large mouth attached to an even larger body and eat a lot! It turns out that when the minkes are in the area, the penguins have to dive deeper, where they switch to eating fish.

When the minkes leave, the penguins switch back to krill. This year, we solve that mystery. It feels good to learn new things.

It is a good, pleasant year at Cape Royds. Weather is mild, food for the penguins is plentiful, and the colony fledges about 1,500 chicks. Joey and Echo are proud parents of two fat, healthy chicks. As we depart for the season, we have a good feeling those chicks will survive their first winter.

I get e-mails and letters asking about Joey and whether he will come back next year. I can only answer, "I don't know," but now there are hundreds of people waiting for Joey.

Chapter 9
A Crack in the Ice
(2015)

Before I leave my home in California and head to Antarctica, I check the satellite images of McMurdo Sound where Cape Royds is located. The images show an unusually large amount of sea ice in the area. Normally, the penguins have to walk at most a few kilometers to their nesting sites at Cape Royds. This year, with ice reaching farther out to sea, it will be more like 60 kilometers (37 miles). Will some birds decide not to walk and go someplace else? We can't wait to find out. Changes in our global climate affect wind patterns, which in turn affect the sea ice. With less wind, the sea ice does not break up as quickly or blow away as fast. This year, we are seeing the results of decreased winds. When we arrive at Cape Royds on November 1, the open ocean is still 60 kilometers (37.2 miles) away.

Penguins are resilient and sturdy birds. They have adapted to the harsh environment of Antarctica, and most of our male Adélies still arrive on time at Cape Royds to build their nests. A few days later, the females show up and lay their eggs. We are smiling, as the breeding cycle appears normal. But where is Joey? Ah, there he is, a few days late, but at least here. Some other males have arrived late as well. It is November 14. Arriving late to build your nest is risky. If eggs are not laid and hatched in time, the chicks will not be large enough to live on their own by the time winter comes. Frequently, late-hatched chicks do not make it.

I am worried about Joey. But undaunted and with full-on breeding energy, Joey makes a nest on the exact same site as last year. And here comes Echo who has also been working her way toward their breeding group. They sing their duet and mate, and soon thereafter Echo lays two eggs. It is November 25, a bit late for egg laying.

Incubating time in the colony is very quiet. All nesting birds are sitting on eggs, there are no wandering birds, and this year it is a long time between parental nest exchanges. The penguins must walk 60 kilometers (37.2 miles) to the open ocean, feed, and then walk the

same distance back before they can relieve their mates. Many of the males have been in the colony since October 28. It is now November 28, one month. Their mates are not back, and these males begin to feel the pangs of hunger more than usual. Something inside of them triggers the "abandon egg" behavior. The hungry males head out of the colony to feed, leaving the eggs to the skuas. Adélie penguins can cover about 8 kilometers (5 miles) per hours swimming and almost that speed tobogganing over the sea ice. They can get to open water—and food—in several hours if they don't stop to rest. Regardless, I hope they have the strength to make the distance to open water and food. Throughout the colony, there are many nests with abandoned eggs, more than the skuas can eat. In a short amount of time, the eggs will freeze, and then the skuas cannot eat them. This loss of eggs is sad, but their fate is evidence that nature can be very dispassionate. Life in Antarctica is a challenge, and there will always be winners and losers.

As the days pass, fewer and fewer nests are left in our colony. Many females do finally return but find their mates and eggs gone; other females we never see again. Some mates, including Echo, do come back in time, and the nest exchanges occur. Joey and the other male penguins hurry to find food before they run out of body fat. Echo took 20 days to make the round trip. She managed to reach open water, find a good source of food and return to change places with Joey. It is Dec 15, the same day our first eggs hatch. In less than 2 weeks their eggs will hatch. Joey doesn't have much time.

The situation becomes more desperate as hatching increases every day. Now the penguins need to make the 60-kilometer (37.2-mile) walk to feed themselves and bring food back to feed the chicks. Nest after nest begins to fail as the tending parent has no food to feed the chicks and the returning parent does not get back in time. The number of chicks in our colony is dwindling rapidly. We have lost over 60 percent of the chicks, and I fear this fate for late-nesting Joey as well.

December 26: Joey's eggs hatch, and there is no sign of Joey. Starvation seems the only outcome, and this saddens us all. His female, Echo, has been waiting patiently for almost two weeks. Then, here comes Joey, over the ice with compelling urgency, a large belly full of food, and just in time to feed two

new mouths attached to hungry bodies. We are amazed at how much he was able to carry back over such a long distance in such a short time. Then I notice another bird with a similar full belly, then another and another. What is going on?

I climb the peak near Cape Royds and look out over the expanse of continuous sea ice. There it is, a large crack about 2 meters (6.7 feet wide) wide stretching from the shore of our island out as far as I can see. The crack starts only 3 kilometers (1.9 miles) from the colony. Wahoo, now there will be plenty of food for the remaining chicks!

Joey's chicks grow fast with the plentiful food supply. Most parents have no chicks to feed, so there is little competition for the krill and fish in the crack,

Ice crack

and the whales can't get to it. When we say good-bye on January 20, Joey's chicks are less than one month old, but fatter than normal, and we feel good about their future. This year, being a late breeder was an advantage. No matter what happens, there are always winners and losers in nature, and what works one year may not work the next. The nature of penguins, though, is to keep trying! As we pack up our equipment and leave Cape Royds to itself for the winter, we are smiling, because even though the colony lost more than 80 percent of its chicks, some will make it. This year, again, Joey was a winner.

Chapter 10
Joey and Echo (2017)

It is my tenth season with the penguin team, and I feel confident in my work, my role on the team, and surviving in Antarctica. Joey is nine years old and a successful parent, a mature adult penguin, and a celebrity. We have grown up in Antarctica together. Returning to Cape Royds, I have no doubt he will also come back. I sit by his nest site daily, waiting to see him come over the hill from the ocean. I am not disappointed: on October 30, here he comes: fat, confident, assured of his purpose and direction. I have choices in my life and think and rethink my decisions, sometimes with agony and inner turmoil. Joey has choices, too, but always goes forward. He knows what he must do and goes directly to his nesting site to begin. He works swiftly to build the nest, and he defends his rocks from other birds that would like to take the easy route and steal rather than gather their own. He then waits for Echo. Life is both simple and difficult for these penguins.

I notice that Joey's feathers are clean, thick, and fluffy. Penguin feathers are more dense than any other bird's. A single square inch (6.45 sq. cm.) holds more than a hundred feathers. In contrast, a chicken would have six in the same area. Because their feathers must keep them warm and dry, penguins preen them daily with oil from the urogial gland located just above their tail. Oiling the feathers keeps them waterproof. Feathers take a beating on the ice and in the cold water. They wear out every year, so penguins must grow new ones (molt) before each winter. Molting happens after the breeding season when the penguins have fed voraciously to regain their condition. The process takes between two and three weeks, and during that time the birds cannot forage for food and will lose weight.

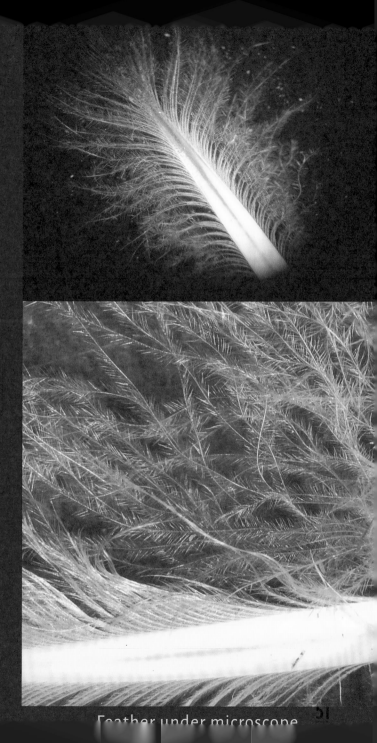

Special Feathers

Penguins are warm blooded animals and have feathers like no other birds. Not big, soft and fluffy, but small, rigid and tight, they are more like the shingles on your roof than a feather pillow. They cover 96% of the bird's body and keep them not only warm, but dry. Even in -50°C temperatures and 60mph winds these birds remain comfortable. In this magnified picture you see the top of the feather, the part we see, which is solid and keeps the penguins dry. It is small but there are thousands and thousands on the bird and they are packed closely together. What we do not see are the downy strands that create the warm air layer next to the birds' skin. Notice the small barbs on the strands that inter-connect with one another to create the dense, tight, dry under-coat. Chick feathers are similar to adult feather except they do not keep the chick dry. They lack the solid contour top. Chicks must wait until they molt into their adult plumage before they can go into the water.

Feather under microscope

Joey's legs are long, and his feet are webbed with very sturdy and sharp toenails to keep him steady on the ice and help him climb over rocks. He is a walking machine. In water, Joey propels himself by using his wings much the way other birds do when flying through the air. He cannot fold his wings like other birds, which makes him better able to move through the water. Joey does not use his feet to paddle like ducks; instead he uses his feet and his tail to help steer while "flying" through the water.

Joey and the other penguins use their strong beaks to catch fish, krill, and squid and swallow their prey whole. Small finger-like projections on their tongue help move the prey toward the back of the mouth in a one-way design that keeps the prey from escaping.

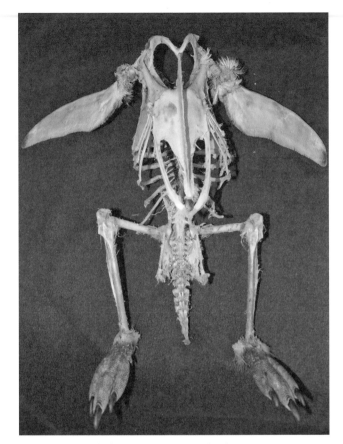
Adélie Penguin skeleton

As we begin our new season, we read about the reduction of Adélie penguin colonies on the northern tip of the Antarctic Peninsula. This area is across the continent from Cape Royds, much further north and near the tip of South America. Here the warming of that region has reduced the amount of sea ice, which is challenging for the Adélies. Adélies never go very far from sea ice because they use these frozen platforms (floes) to rest on as they forage for food. Their association with sea ice is similar to the way other birds live in trees and find food there or on the ground. If you cut down the trees, these birds will disappear. The Adélie populations in the northern Antarctic Peninsula area have been disappearing with the ice. Many have moved to locations where the conditions remain suitable for them.

Chinstrap penguins

Adélie penguins can store large amounts of fat, which they live on when the sea ice covers the ocean, since feeding is difficult and they are required to fast. Other penguins don't store fat as well so need to be in places where the open ocean is more accessible. Adélies can also hold their breath longer than other penguins in the area and are able to forage under large ice floes. This makes the Adélies well suited for regions largely covered with ice. Other penguin species, the gentoo and chinstrap, stay away from the sea ice as much as they can. Their populations have increased with the reduction of sea ice in the northern Antarctic Peninsula region. Remember, there are always winners and losers in nature. For us at Cape Royds, much farther to the south, plenty of sea ice remains. Although we have seen changes in the climate, it is still cold enough to maintain the ice floe coverage needed to keep our penguins happy.

Gentoo penguins

54

On November 3, here comes Echo. She, too, is fat and sleek, and she moves quickly to unite with her long-term mate, Joey. Eggs appear by November 10, and now 500 classrooms are watching to see how this breeding season unfolds for our penguin pair.

On December 20, Joey is foraging for his two lovely chicks. One of the chicks, energetically exploring its space, moves too close to the edge of the nest. A sharp-eyed skua overhead notices this fatal move and swoops down. Echo cannot react in time, and the chick is taken by the skua. When Joey returns, there is only one chick left in the nest. This saddens me, but Echo exhibits total calm and acceptance. I receive many e-mails and cards from students who are also feeling this loss. The cycle of life in the colony can seem cruel, but all the animals depend on the others for their food, and this event is a natural one.

I am doing between six and eight Skype calls a day from my place near Joey and Echo's nest. Two thousand children have watched these parents raise their family again one more year.

This year, our research team will explore where these birds go in the winter. We select Joey to wear a special band around his leg. The band has an electronic device that will record where he goes and his feeding behavior—how many dives he takes and the depth of his dives for the entire winter. The leg band is very small and will not interfere with his swimming. For us to retrieve the data, Joey will have to return to Cape Royds next year and let us remove the band. He has shown himself to be faithful to Cape Royds and his mate, so we look forward to finding him here next year. One more mystery we want to unravel.

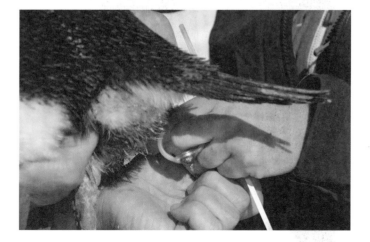

On January 16, we leave Cape Royds and say good-bye to Joey and Echo. Their single chick is very robust, one of the biggest in the colony. He will do well this winter season, because we have learned that large, fat chicks have the best chance to survive, and we hope to see him in a few years. Joey is wearing our geolocator, and now more than 2,000 people, including me, are waiting for Joey to return.

GLOSSARY

Adélie penguin Small penguin 46 centimeters (1.5 feet) tall that always lives where there is sea ice, but builds its nests of rocks on coastal land in Antarctica. Named after Adèle Dumont D'Urville, the wife of explorer Jules Dumont D'Urville. Scientific name: Pygoscelis adeliae.

Antarctic The fifth largest continent on Earth. Almost completely covered with ice and snow and surrounded by the Southern Ocean.

Banding Method of identifying individual birds by placing a numbered band on either their leg or wing.

Breeding colony Group of penguins that come together for the purpose of raising their chicks. Colonies can be small, with several hundred penguins, or large, with several hundred thousand.

Breeding season November to February for Adélie penguins. Summertime in Antarctica and the time frame for these penguins to complete the raising of their chicks.

Brood, brooding Time span when adult penguins are either sitting on eggs or caring for very small chicks.

Brood patch Featherless place on the penguin's belly just big enough to snuggle two eggs. Eggs must be held next to the skin to gain warmth from the bird's body.

Chick Young penguin from the time it hatches until it swims off to sea.

Chinstrap penguin	Similar in size to the Adélie penguin, this penguin breeds in the Subantarctic islands and on the Antarctic peninsula. Scientific name: Pygoscelis antarcticus.
Colony	Group of breeding penguins.
Courtship display	A bird's behavior intended to attract a mate.
Crèche	Group of chicks that are too large to stay in the nest but not ready to swim off. These chicks still have their downy feathers and need to huddle together to stay warm.
Data loggers	Small electronic devices used to collect data remotely.
Guard stage	Time span when adult penguins are very close to the nest and chicks, but chicks are too large to be brooded.
Fledgling	Chick that has left the colony, swum out to sea, and is now independent of its parents.
Foraging	Searching for food. Adélie penguins swim both under the ice and in open water looking for krill, squid, and small fish.
Gentoo penguin	Similar in size to the Adélie penguin, this penguin breeds in the Subantarctic islands and on the Antarctic peninsula. Scientific name: Pygoscelis papua.
Geolocator	Small data logger attached to a penguin's leg that records the movement of the bird.
Hydrodynamic	Refers to a shape that allows water to flow over it easily. Penguin wings are very hydrodynamic, allowing them to swim at great speeds underwater.
Ice floes	Pieces of floating sea ice. They can be a yard to several miles across, completely flat or a crumpled jumble of large pieces. Some are salty ice; some are pure water.

Ice sheet	Another name for a continental glacier, or a broad expanse of snow turned to ice. In the Antarctic and Greenland, ice sheets are more than 2 kilometers (1.2 miles) thick. The three major ice sheets in the world are the West Antarctic Ice Sheet, the East Antarctic Ice Sheet, and the Greenland Ice Sheet. The West Antarctic Ice Sheet is the most vulnerable to global warming because it is resting on the seafloor. A rise in sea level will cause it to float and go away, causing the sea level to rise even more.
Krill	Norwegian word meaning "whale food." Refers to small, 6-centimeter (2.4-inch) shrimp-like creatures that live in schools, with as many as 19 million per square kilometer (0.4 square mile). The dominant species in offshore waters of the southern polar oceans is the Antarctic krill, Euphausia superba, which can live from five to ten years; the dominant species in coastal waters is called ice or crystal krill, E. crystallorophias. Krill eat phytoplankton, which grows near the surface of the ocean and under the ice. Females lay 10,000 eggs at a time and may lay several times per season.
Minke whale	Baleen whale that eats krill, usually 7 to 8 meters (21-25 feet) long.
Molt	To replace old feathers with new ones. Penguins cannot swim during this time so must fast.
Natal	Refers to the site area or colony where a bird was hatched.
National Science Foundation	US funding agency that provides grants to scientists across a large range of topics.
Orca	Largest member of the dolphin family found in all the world's oceans. Common name: killer whale; scientific name: Orcinus orca.
Predation, predator	An interaction between two species where the predator organism feeds on another living organism or organisms known as prey.
Preen	To groom the feathers, keeping them clean and in place.

Recognition song	Vocalization between penguins. Used for recognition among mates and parents and chicks.
Regurgitate	To vomit. Adult penguins feed their chicks by regurgitating food from their stomachs into the mouth of their chicks.
Resilient	Able to recover quickly from adversity or challenges.
Ross Sea	A deep sea of the Southern Ocean in Antarctica, between Victoria Land and Marie Byrd Land. It derives its name from the British explorer James Ross who visited this area in 1841.
Scavengers	Animals that feed on dead or decaying animals.
Sea ice	Ice formed from the freezing of ocean water.
Skua	Large, noisy, and aggressive bird that nests near penguin colonies. In addition to eating fish, krill, and squid, skuas prey on penguin eggs and chicks. Scientific name: Stercorarius maccormicki.
Solar panel	Group of solar cells connected together to generate electricity from the sun.
Subadult	Stage of life between chick and adult. Penguin subadults are on their own but not mature enough to breed.
Synchronous	Refers to a species' breeding season. Those with low synchrony may lay their eggs anytime throughout a lengthy period, from four months to continuously throughout the year. Those with high synchrony, such as Adélie penguins, all create their nests and lay their eggs within a narrow time frame of six days to one month.
Territory	Small nesting area a penguin defends against other penguins or intruders.
Uropygial gland	Gland located near the base of the tail on most bird species. Penguins use the oil from the gland to preen their feathers, keeping them clean and waterproof.

FURTHER READING

Armstrong, Jennifer. *Shipwreck at the Bottom of the World*. New York: Crown, 2000.

Atwater, Richard, and Florence Atwater. *Mr. Popper's Penguins*. Boston: Little, Brown, 1992.

Chester, Jonathan. *The Nature of Penguins*. Berkeley, CA: Celestial Arts, 2001.

Cole, Carol A. *The Penguin Lady*. Mount Pleasant, SC: Sylvan Dell, 2012.

Davis, Lloyd S. *The Plight of the Penguin*. Dunedin, New Zealand: Longacre Press, 2001.

Davis, Lloyd Spencer. *A Season in the Life of an Adélie Penguin*. New York: Harcourt Children's Books, 1994.

———. *Smithsonian Q & A: Penguins*. New York: Harper Perennial, 2007.

Jacquet, Luc, *March of the Penguins*. Washington, DC: National Geographic Children's Books, 2005.

McKnight, Diane, *The Lost Seal*. Lafayette, CO: Moonlight Publishing, 2006.

Richardson, Justin, and Peter Parneff, *And Tango Makes Three*. New York: Simon & Schuster, 2005.

Simon, Seymour. *Penguins*. New York: Collins, 2009.

Webb, Sophie, *My Season with Penguins*. New York: Houghton Mifflin, 2000.

For updates on Joey's return to Cape Royds,
come visit the Waiting for Joey web page at
http://www.penguinscience.com/classroom_home.php

For more information about studying penguins in Antarctica,
please visit the project website at
http://www.penguinscience.com/

The Adélie penguin research project described in this book
is supported by
The National Science Foundation
grants # 0610122, #0732502, #0944411, #1141948, #1543541

ABOUT THE AUTHOR

Jean Pennycook has traveled to Antarctica 17 times providing educational outreach for science projects funded through the National Science Foundation. For the last 13 austral seasons she has worked with the Adélie penguin team at Cape Royds sharing the wonders of penguins, Antarctica and scientific research with children around the world.

Jean has a degree in Wildlife and Fisheries Biology, and a Master's in Science Education. She lives in California.

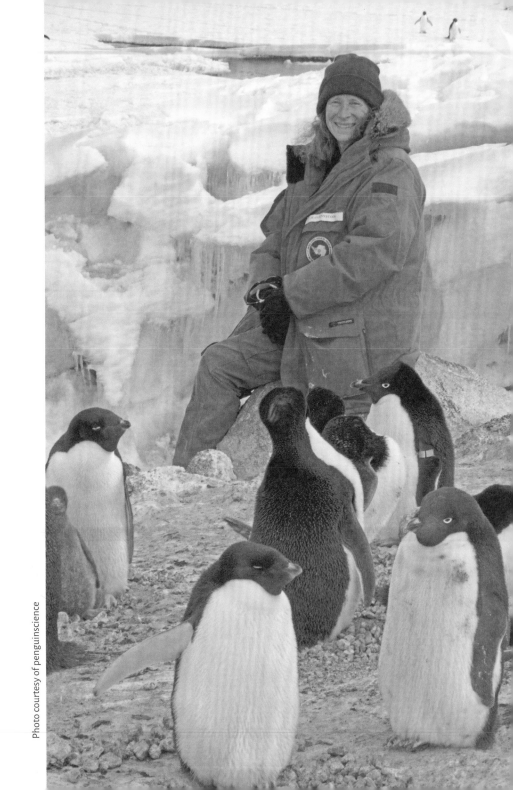

Photo courtesy of penguinscience

64